JOE WELLS

COMPLETE

*BECOMING THE MAN
GOD PURPOSES YOU TO BE*

KAIO PUBLICATIONS, INC.

Complete: Becoming the Man God Purposes You to Be

Copyright © 2022
Joe Wells

Published by Kaio Publications
http://www.kaiopublications.org

Printed and Bound in the
United States of America
All Rights Reserved

Scripture taken from the NEW AMERICAN STANDARD BIBLE
Copyright © 1960, 1962, 1963, 1968, 1971, 1972, 1973, 1975, 1977 by the Lockman Foundation.
Used by permission.

ISBN: 978-1-952955-39-6

All rights reserved. No portion of this book may be reproduced in any form without the written permission of the author or publisher, including translation.

TABLE OF CONTENTS

INTRODUCTION 1

CHAPTER 1: LESSONS FROM **THE BLESSED MAN** 3

CHAPTER 2: LESSONS FROM **THE JUSTIFIED MAN** 15

CHAPTER 3: LESSONS FROM **THE WISE MAN** 27

CHAPTER 4: LESSONS FROM **THE HUMBLE MAN** 39

CHAPTER 5: LESSONS FROM **THE PATIENT MAN** 51

ENDNOTES 63

INTRODUCTION

"Consider it all joy, my brethren, when you encounter various trials, knowing that the testing of your faith produces endurance. And let endurance have its perfect result, so that you may be perfect and complete, lacking in nothing."

- James 1: 2-4 -

What is your goal?

I don't mean today or tomorrow. I'm talking about your goal that overrides all your milestones and the one that stands above all and is constantly before your mind's eyes as you evaluate your life. While we all have incremental goals and steps toward success we outline, these pale in comparison when we genuinely contemplate the success of our lives according to how close we are getting to this one main goal.

Whatever your verbal answer to this question, your life's direction and aim will unapologetically and unabashedly reveal the truth. If financial gain is your goal, but your actions don't involve getting to work on time and putting in the effort, then your goal isn't really financial gain. If health is your goal, but you never cut back on what you eat nor exercise, your real goal isn't to get healthy. Instead, these are dreams, thoughts that would be wonderful but not ones that ever become a reality. It's like brainstorming for direction but never launching and heading down the path to get you there. Many live their lives with dreams instead of goals.

Please don't get the impression that I'm suggesting dreaming is not needed or has zero positive benefits. I'm not saying that. However, having an abstract thought or concept float through our minds as we think about what could be is very different from having a clear direction and aim. Once we set goals, we have moved from the realm of possibility into the arena of reality. We know where we want to go; therefore, we are in a much better position to work toward such. When financial gain becomes a goal instead of a dream, your life will demonstrate behavior and actions to reach that end. The same is valid with health or any number of goals you set. Goals offer a more concrete direction and allow for mapping steps to reach the desired result.

Complete: Becoming the Man God Purposes You to Be is written with a goal-oriented mindset, not a dream. A loving God would not desire completeness or maturity if such were not obtainable. That's why this book is written with the default conclusion that becoming complete, while a lifelong journey and endeavor, by the grace of God and His work in our lives, is possible.

Men, as you dive into this study of the men of James, I encourage you to make personal application. Read, not merely to gain information; instead, I ask that as you read, you consider your personal goal, the big one in this life, of becoming the man God purposes you to become. It is a lifelong journey that will always be a pursuit if we're being completely honest with ourselves. That's the way it is with maturity and wholeness. We continually die to ourselves and live for Him (Matthew 16:24). We are not dwelling on our past accomplishments or failures. Instead, we are striving or "pressing on" toward our goal of completeness in the eyes of God (Philippians 3:12).

I pray that those who courageously take on this life-long endeavor, this continual journey toward completeness, would be blessed by Almighty God as we strive to decrease in selfish pursuits and increase in wholeness according to God's revealed will.

- Joe

LESSONS FROM
THE BLESSED MAN

———

"Blessed is the man who perseveres under trial; for once he has been approved, he will receive the crown of life which the Lord has promised to those who love Him."

- James 1:12 -

INTRODUCTION

When I was in college, a group of men from the congregation I was attending decided we would venture into the rugged terrain of middle Tennessee on a great hiking adventure. We were to explore the area called "Savage Gulf," so you could imagine my gleeful anticipation of the exhaustion I fully expected. With the plan being that we would spend two nights and three days along the trail, everything we needed had to be packed in and the garbage packed out, as we knew we did not need to leave any trace or impact on the environment. That meant we had to be meticulous in what we brought. There is no way possible that one man could carry everything, so after collectively coming together with all the food, cooking supplies, tents, and so forth, we divided the weight between backpacks. The plan was that each man would put his personal belongings and the group's items in the bag. If you wanted a lot, you would be carrying a lot; however, after the initial distribution of necessities, the weight of your pack was literally on your shoulders.

The trip was fantastic! Even though I had never done anything like that before, this inexperienced young college kid was able to complete the treacherous daily hikes and enjoy nights of climbing into my sleeping bag in the day's filth. No doubt, it was a younger man's activity and one I'm glad

I experienced; however, now that I have my children and reflect on this incredible expedition, I can't help but more clearly see the potential dangers. With a different perspective, I am faced with the reality that if we had not had our friend Cade on that trip, there is no telling what pitfalls could have occurred. He was the only one of us who had any experience in the field, and we relied heavily upon him.

Let me explain.

On the last day of the hike, we were low on supplies, which was expected and potentially helpful because the more we ate, the lighter the backpacks became. However, it was only a partial positive because one of the depleted items was water. In the years since the trip, and with my growing inability to remember as I used to, I can't recall why we ran low on water. All I remember is that drinking water boiled in a camp pot that had a residue of chicken grease from the night before is awful. Yet, when I reflect on how dehydration might have felt in the middle of a lovely place called "Savage Gulf," the chicken grease water wasn't so bad.

Cade entered the picture with this horrible dilemma to solve. With his experience of taking numerous excursions like this, he could draw from the wisdom he had gained. We didn't have fancy purifying drinking straws, and the water purification pills were not an option on this trip. So as we approached a tiny stream of water, Cade collected enough in a container and started a fire. He boiled the water in the pot, the nasty chicken grease pot, so we all had a ration to quench our immediate thirst. It was Cade's quick thinking and proper knowledge that led him to show us the way to have drinkable water, without which I believe several of us would have suffered from dehydration.

Having someone who has "been there, done that" to mentor you and lead the way can be a tremendous asset when venturing through a beastly place like Savage Gulf. Cade proved to be irreplaceable. We wanted to complete the course and get out of the woods. He had successfully accomplished this before and knew what it would take, and we were more than happy to follow his lead.

The same holds true when the conversation is about the spiritual excursion that all of humanity is walking, one that has far greater consequences than merely physical dehydration or hunger. This venture is genuinely about eternal life or eternal damnation, and it's about the grace God freely gives to the humble or the judgment to be rendered to the self-righteous. That's why it's so crucial for those of us who seek the crown of life to look to those in Scripture who know what it is like to be approved of God.

In James chapter 1, we find such an individual; however, this faithful person is not known by name. We simply know him as the Blessed Man (James 1:12). What we glean of him is based upon his standing before God, being one who is approved of God and who is promised to receive the glorious crown of life. He is firmly planted in the category of those who love God and are committed to continually enduring, persevering, and leaning on God as they faithfully journey in life. In a spiritual sense, these are the ones who serve as mentors, just as Cade did in a physical way on the tiresome trip through Savage Gulf. This Blessed Man of James 1:12 is our example. We want what he has; therefore, we are committed to diligently understanding and mirroring what he has done and continues to do along the journey.

THE BLESSED MAN...

1) PERSEVERES UNDER TRIAL

No one likes to feel discomfort or pain. Like me, you will likely take calculated measures to avoid such. We do this because we all hold a sense of self-preservation and regularly put it into practice. This is understandable when we're talking about chopping wood and making sure we arrange the area so that we won't be tripped by rolling pieces of wood. It's beneficial when we are cooking and want to make sure we grab the potholder before touching the iron skillet's handle, preventing a sizzling effect on the bare skin of our hands. It's also a good character trait when staying alert when driving a car, cutting with a knife, starting a fire in the firepit, and even mowing the yard. We take extra measures to avoid pitfalls because we want to avoid as much discomfort as possible.

However, this need for self-preservation can sometimes be a tremendous obstacle we must face head-on. When a difficult conversation must be had, some flock toward the debate and others hurriedly run the other way, desiring to avoid the uncomfortable situation. Some do the same when it comes to religious discussions, especially those where family is involved and disagreements are known before the first word is ever unchained. Self-preservation is also in full force when it comes to peer pressure, job pressure, spousal pressure, and any number of vice-oriented stressors that occur in our daily lives. Some will face them as David did Goliath, while others allow the need to escape the uncomfortable to take over.

In James 1:12, we learn that the Blessed Man is the one who "perseveres under trial."

- perseveres under" - υπομενει (*hupomenei*) -

  This is a combination of two Greek words: hupó (under) and ménō (to remain) and refers to one's response in the face of highly uncomfortable and challenging circumstances.[1] The tense of the word denotes a continual action; thus, this is not a one-time "getting through a rough spot" concept, and it describes someone who is choosing to remain under a difficult circumstance as an ongoing way of living.

  In chapter 5, verse 11, James highlights Job as an example of enduring extreme trial. "We count those blessed who endured. You have heard of the endurance (NKJV uses the word "perseverance") of Job and have seen the outcome of the Lord's dealings, that the Lord is full of compassion and is merciful." Such an example draws one back to Job 1:21 when, in response to the news of the death of his family, Job said, "Naked I came from my mother's womb, and naked I shall return there. The Lord gave and the Lord has taken away. Blessed be the name of the Lord." Job's refusal to turn his back on God when difficulties and pain arose in his family, and to him personally, serves as an accurate picture of what it means to choose to faithfully remain under tremendous hardship.

- "trial" - πειρασμός (*peirasmós*) -

  This word means "to make trial of, try, tempt."[2] When God is the agent of the trial, it is always to prove one's character and faith, and it's never to cause an individual to fall. In contrast, if the devil is the acting agent, then the purpose is always to cause one to sin.

  We see this same word used in James 1:2-3 when we read, "Consider it all joy, my brethren, when you encounter various trials, knowing that the testing of your faith produces endurance." Thus, the perseverance of the Blessed Man of 1:12 is to be understood within his immediate context. In the opening of this letter, James boldly introduces the concept of looking through the lens of faith when it comes to the trials Christians face in this life. What is impressive about this Blessed Man is that he makes a purposeful and intellectual choice to positively see the difficult circumstances in this life. James never wrote that he would enjoy the trial; however, he did point his audience to the disposition and long-term outcome of such trials. The more he chose to remain under the burden, the more endurance was produced. Endurance begets more perseverance which eventually results in the maturity of faith. The Blessed Man of James 1 is the one who faithfully remains under the weight for the totality of the trial. He doesn't run from it. Instead, he embraces it and keeps his focus narrowed on walking with God.

> *He considers the opportunity to grow in his endurance through difficult trials as a chance to rejoice, not as an excuse to complain.*

What's extraordinary about the Blessed Man is that he does not take the easy way out. Self-preservation does not cause him to run and hide from what is painful and arduous. Instead, he determines to focus on the benefit and not the burden. He considers the opportunity to grow in his endurance through difficult trials as a chance to rejoice, not as an excuse to complain. Consequently, his faith is fortified, not forfeited, and it's mature, not microscopic.

2) ACCEPTS OWNERSHIP OF HIS SIN

Excuses…Dismissal…Blame

During our lives many of us may have used these three tactics to avoid accepting responsibility. Growing up with two brothers, I remember when we were told to accomplish a task our parents had assigned. We knew what was expected and the timeframe for completion. As brothers, we would "divide" the task into smaller jobs. Our thought was that if we all did our part, the considerable chore would be accomplished in a timely manner. However, there were times when one of us may not have finished his job or at least didn't get it done in time. Then there would be an uncomfortable conversation when Dad and Mom got home. Usually, as soon as our failure to get the job done was pointed out, we would immediately begin pointing fingers at the one who didn't get his job done. He would then point his finger back at the other two, who probably disproportionately divided the task. No matter what excuse was given, I remember my father was very consistent. He and my mother assigned the task, not the job divisions. That was something we did; therefore, although two may have completed their tasks, we all received the punishment if the whole assignment wasn't done.

Just as there is a great consequence to making excuses, dismissing fault, and blaming others for our physical behaviors, there are even more severe ramifications for refusing to take ownership of sins we commit. King Saul is a perfect example of someone who tried to dismiss personal sin and cast blame. In 1 Samuel 13, when the massive Philistine army was assembled for battle against the Israelites, and the men with Saul began to flee because they were intimidated and scared, we read how Saul disobeyed the will of God by offering the sacrifice that was supposed to be made by Samuel. In doing so, Saul sinned. He could have repented and offered sacrifice for his sin; however, when Samuel confronted him, he began blaming others, saying, "Because I saw that the people were scattering from me, and that you did not come within the appointed days , and that the Philistines were assembling at Michmash, therefore I said, 'Now the Philistines will come down against me at Gilgal, and I have not asked the favor of the Lord.' So I forced myself and offered the burnt offering" (vv. 11-12). As a result of his sin and his lack of ownership of his actions, Samuel told him that his kingdom would not endure (v. 14).

In turning our attention to the Blessed Man of James in chapter 1, we are led to conclude that this man responds in a way that is the opposite of Saul. He does take ownership of his decisions and his behavior. We draw this from a stern warning put forth by James when he writes, "Let no one say when he is tempted, 'I am being tempted by God'; for God cannot be tempted by evil, and He Himself does not tempt anyone. But each one is tempted when he is carried away and enticed by his own lust. Then when lust has conceived, it gives birth to sin; and when sin is accomplished, it brings forth death" (vv.

13-15). James reveals a dangerous belief held by some in his time that God is the one who tempts. After all, if God is in control of all things, He must also be the one who draws humanity to evil deeds. James debunks that myth by explaining that God is the great gift-giver of all things good (v. 17). He reminds these Christians how the Father of Lights called us by the Word of truth to be redeemed (vv. 17-18).

While many try to slide by with sin, always presenting a "reason" why it is someone else's fault or why they were compelled to act that way, the reality is that it's all a lie. The sinful attitudes, dispositions, thoughts, and actions in our lives are our fault. In following the logic of James 1:14-15, our desires move us in the directions we already wanted to go. Temptations abound because Satan is no beginner in ensnaring humanity (1 Timothy 3:7; 2 Timothy 2:26); however, the fact that temptation is presented doesn't mean a person must move in the direction of the lure. We can choose what we will give in to and what we will resist. When we give in to our desires toward a temptation, spiritual death is the outcome (James 1:15).

The Blessed Man knows this and doesn't seek to pass the blame or dismiss personal responsibility. He is not looking to merely appear right in the eyes of men. Instead, the Blessed Man desires to be right with God. To do so, he must take personal ownership of his sin and repent, seeking the mercy of the gracious God (James 4:6).

3) IS AN EFFECTUAL DOER, NOT MERELY A HEARER

The COVID-19 pandemic of 2020 was nothing short of life changing. History will reveal that this was a time of great confusion, political spin, and divisive rhetoric. Congregations were faced with all kinds of rules and regulations from the state governments. Some even mandated that congregations could not meet, and others dictated that congregations could not sing during services. Elders were faced with shepherding the flock through extremely rough waters. Social distancing became a slogan visibly displayed in just about every grocery store; stickers on the floor showing where to stand to keep the six feet of separation between you and the customer in front of you were a regular sight. It was, and most likely will continue to be, a very odd and confusing time.

Part of the confusion that has been rampant during this time is the changing narrative regarding the virus and its spread. At one time, we were told masks were not effective in decreasing the spread of the virus. Then we were told masks were needed, that we needed two masks at one time, and that the only genuinely effective mask against the spread of COVID-19 were N95 masks. On top of that, we were told that if we all just stayed inside our homes for about 15 days, the virus would disappear because that's how long people who had COVID-19 remained contagious. Then we found out that wasn't the case. We were told that all those who encountered someone who had symptoms of the virus needed to quarantine for two weeks; then that changed to a lower number. Those who had the virus only needed to quarantine for ten days after the symptoms subsided. Then that was changed to five days. Then, for front-line workers (emergency medical personnel), the quarantine period could be ignored because of the shortage of workers in the hospitals. Schools were closed as children began schooling virtually. Office buildings were closed as Zoom meetings became the norm. Even outdoor sporting events restricted fans from attending.

As a result of the changing narrative, suspicions of the top governing officials making the mandates increased. Many Americans began dismissing everything the head of the World Health Organization said. There were calls for the resignation of the National Institute of Allergy and Infectious Diseases (NIAID) director and the chief medical advisor to the president. Politicians alienated constituents as they began to use the pandemic to advance their political agendas. Americans continued to grow weary. The majority of them had abided by what they were told, but the confusion caused many to begin to ignore the words of those who were supposed to be "taking care" of the pandemic.

> ...the Blessed Man is the one who reveres the One behind the Word.

An integral component of a listener's response is confidence in the one speaking. The pandemic of 2020 taught us a lot; however, one of the biggest lessons was that when you can't trust the messenger, the message begins to fall on deaf ears. The opposite of this is also true. When the source of the words can be trusted, the weight of his words is more likely to be carried. In our text, the Blessed Man is the one who reveres the One behind the Word. Because he does respect God, he acts according to the Word. Thus, the Blessed Man of James 1 is a doer of the Word of God, not merely one who shows up on Sunday to listen to the sermon.

To demonstrate this, please consider with me how God is described in James chapter 1:

- James 1:5 - **The One Who Answers Prayers of Faith**

    "But if any of you lacks wisdom, let him ask of God, who gives to all generously and without reproach, and it will be given to him."

- James 1:12 - **The One Who is Faithful to His Promises**

    "Blessed is the man who perseveres under trial; for once he has been approved, he will receive the crown of life which the Lord has promised to those who love Him."

- James 1:13 - **The One Who Cannot and Does Not Tempt Anyone to Evil**

    "Let no one say when he is tempted, 'I am being tempted by God'; for God cannot be tempted by evil, and He Himself does not tempt anyone."

- James 1:17 - **The One Who Gives Every Good Thing**

    "Every good thing given and every perfect gift is from above, coming down from the Father of lights, with whom there is no variation or shifting shadow."

- James 1:17 - **The One Who Is Consistent**

    "Every good thing given and every perfect gift is from above, coming down from the Father of lights, with whom there is no variation or shifting shadow."

- James 1:18 - **The One Who Brings the Spiritual Dead to Life**

    "In the exercise of His will He brought us forth by the word of truth, so that we would be a kind of first fruits among His creatures."

- James 1:18 - **The One Who is the Creator**

    "In the exercise of His will He brought us forth by the word of truth, so that we would be a kind of first fruits among His creatures."

- James 1:20 - **The One Who is the Standard of Righteousness**

"For the anger of man does not achieve the righteousness of God."

- James 1:27 - **The One Who Defines Pure and Undefiled Religion**

"Pure and undefiled religion in the sight of our God and Father is this: to visit orphans and widows in their distress, and to keep oneself unstained by the world."

It is fascinating and beneficial to see the various ways God is described in this one chapter. We would do ourselves a disservice to glaze over them. In them we see the reasons James, by inspiration of the Holy Spirit, gives for leaning into God by trusting Him enough to align one's life with His Word, defined as "the word of truth" (1:18) and the "word implanted, which is able to save your souls" (1:21). God is worthy of not merely our attention but our trust. He is the Creator, Sustainer, Deliverer, Prayer Answerer, Gift Giver, and the only Constant that never changes. That's why you should trust and obey what He says. That's what the Blessed Man does. He chooses to:

- James 1:19 - be quick to listen to the Word
- James 1:19 - be slow to speak regarding the Word
- James 1:19 - be slow to become angered because of the Word
- James 1:21 - put aside all moral impurity
- James 1:21 - put aside all that remains of evil or depravity in his life
- James 1:21 - receive the Word deliberately and readily
- James 1:22 - display through faithful action his receptiveness to the Word
- James 1:22 - refuse to deceive himself by thinking merely hearing the Word is enough
- James 1:25 - look intently into the perfect law, the law of liberty
- James 1:25 - abide by the law of liberty
- James 1:25 - be an effectual doer of the perfect law

As we consider this aspect of the Blessed Man of James chapter 1, we should not move on without considering what is meant by being a doer and not merely a hearer of the Word. The terrifying constant of these categories is that hearing the Word takes place by both the hearer and the doer. This means that even the hearer shows up to worship and is present when the preacher delivers the sermon. The hearer sits in a Bible class when the Word of God is taught. He may even make comments in class. However, the difference between the hearer and the doer could not be more serious. While the hearer shows up, he does not live out what he has heard and studied. For the hearer, it's become more of an intellectual exercise that stops at the door of the church building. However, the one who is like the Blessed Man, the effectual doer of the Word, daily lives not merely studying God's Word but implementing the Word of truth with every step he takes, every day of every week.

> *While the hearer shows up, he does not live out what he has heard and studied.*

CONCLUSION

As Cade led us through Savage Gulf, I must admit that even though he was an older teenager and I was a college student, I looked to his example to navigate the journey. After all, I had been more interested in sports and hanging out with friends than I had in trekking through the forest on paths designed for people who were in much better physical shape than I. He had the experience, and I wanted to gain the knowledge and practical understanding to not only escape the woods after three days but to enjoy the journey along the way.

The Blessed Man of James chapter 1 stands in the same place; however, his example is more consequential. In James 1:12, we read, "Blessed is the man who perseveres under trial; for once he has been approved, he will receive the crown of life which the Lord has promised to those who love Him." The Blessed Man has what we want, the approval of God and the crown of life. If we genuinely want what he has, we must do what he does. That's the bottom line of this chapter. In a sense, the Blessed Man is the guide along the trail. He is the one who's "been there, done that." If we want to not only faithfully reach the end of the path but enjoy the journey along the way, we must follow his lead.

REFLECTION QUESTIONS

1. Self-preservation is a necessary part of living; however, how can this become a struggle for you as you grow in your faith?
2. Conflict is not fun. However, at times, it's necessary. When you sin (Romans 3:23), what are some real-life hindrances to taking ownership of your sin and even seeking forgiveness if you have sinned against another?
3. What freedom is there in attempting to pass the guilt for your sin on to another?
4. Maturing is a process that occurs over a lifetime. As you grow in your knowledge of God and your absolute trust in Him, how will that be revealed in your life? In your marriage? In your parenting? In your grandparenting? At work?

LESSONS FROM
THE JUSTIFIED MAN

"You see that a man is justified by works and not by faith alone."

- James 2:24 -

INTRODUCTION

I love science - actual science, that is. I don't care at all for the historical/revisionist pseudo-science taught by many today. What I mean by science is the "knowledge about or study of the natural world based on facts learned through experiments and observation."[1] It's the simple desire to explain what can be observed and tested that draws many of us because we long to answer the questions *why*, *how*, and *what*. Why does light look like it does? How are rainbows formed? What causes some storm systems to turn deadly while others simply water the yard? These may seem like elementary questions to many; however, we all pondered these thoughts and many others like them at some point in our lives.

One area of science that has always intrigued me is physics. Perhaps it's because I like understanding the impact of interaction. I am drawn to try to understand interactions with others in my life and especially with those I am trying to help in ministry. We know we do not exist within a figurative bubble; therefore, we are constantly interacting and reacting to our environment and to the people who inhabit that environment. Physics is similar in that it's the study that "deals with matter and energy and the way they act on each other in heat, light, electricity, and sound."[2] Physics operates with laws that are consistent and dependable. The law of gravity exists even if I can't see it. Everything thrown up into the air falls back to the ground unless there is a force acting upon the object that overpowers gravity—like a drone that is cast into the air and the propellers are engaged as it is on the way up.

Another law of physics that falls under the umbrella of Sir Isaac Newton's laws of motion is the law of inertia, the first law. Building off the work of Galileo Galilei, an Italian philosopher, astronomer, and mathematician, Newton successfully tested and concluded that "an object will continue to be in the state of rest or a state of motion unless an external force acts on it."[3] This is not a complicated concept when one considers how this is revealed every day in straightforward ways. A baseball will stay at rest unless a force more significant than the ball's mass acts upon it. So a baseball pitcher throws the ball, the ball moves. A batter hits the ball, and the motion of the ball is redirected and goes into the field of play. All of this demonstrates the law of inertia. Another common way this law is shown is when a person standing inside a bus is propelled backward when the bus begins to move forward. He does so because there is a force acting on his body; until his body "catches up" with the force of the movement of the bus, this reaction is observed.

I want you to stop and think for a minute about these and other laws of physics. Do these laws exist even if they are not visible? In other words, is the law of gravity present even when no one is demonstrating or testing it in the laboratory? Your answer should be, "Yes, because the law of gravity is always in place." If that is your answer, you are correct. What about the law of inertia? The same could be said. Even when I don't see an experiment demonstrating these laws, the rules are still in existence and are constantly in effect. That's the nature of the laws. With every body movement, rocking of a chair, lifting of a coffee cup, throwing of a ball, pushing of a button on a remote control, sending of a text, and any number of other movements and motions you and I engage in daily without thinking about them, we demonstrate these laws. That's because there is no such thing as the law of gravity or inertia without a demonstration of such. They are so interconnected and intertwined that it is impossible to have the law without demonstrating that law.

In James chapter 2, we find the same concept regarding one's faith.

> *What use is it, my brethren, if someone says he has faith but he has no works? Can that faith save him? If a brother or sister is without clothing and in need of daily food, and one of you says to them, "Go in*

peace, be warmed and be filled," and yet you do not give them what is necessary for their body, what use is that? Even so faith, if it has no works, is dead, being by itself. (James 2:14-17)

As James addresses the subject of faith (used 16 times in chapter 2 alone), he drives home the effect of a useless faith (2:20) versus a perfected faith (2:22). The futile faith claims to exist yet has no tangible demonstration of its existence. Conversely, the perfected faith lives in the constant presence of works that demonstrate that faith is present. One, the useless faith, "cannot save" (2:14) and "is dead" (2:17, 26). The perfected faith, however, has a track record of "working with his works" (2:22) and "justifies" (2:24).

Within this discussion of faith, we find our second character, the Justified Man, the man who is deemed righteous by God. Like the Blessed Man of chapter 1, the Justified Man is a Christian who is reliant upon God. He trusts God in all things and is a doer of the Word. He is not a pew warmer; instead, he is a fired-up disciple of Jesus Christ. He does not hold to the belief that his works merit salvation. However, he also understands that "faith without works" is a dead and useless faith (2:20).

THE JUSTIFIED MAN...

1) LOOKS AT PEOPLE THE WAY GOD LOOKS AT PEOPLE - WITHOUT PARTIALITY

He looked the part. He was a warrior who had served in the military and had been trained in combat. He had a dedication, a sense of duty, and a desire to obey. Growing up, he was the oldest son in his family, meaning he would one day inherit a double portion and assume the leadership role within the family. Time and energy had been poured into him by those responsible for rearing him. He was crafted for this, and the one who was sent to select this prominent servant even assumed he was to be anointed; however, Samuel was instructed to pass over Eliab and anoint the brother least likely to be chosen, David, as king (1 Samuel 16:6-7).

She was not the best role model in the city, as everyone was aware. If men were looking for immoral activity, she was willing to provide. They knew where to go—her house. She lived in the city wall, which indicates she was not one of the elites within the inner fortification. Most would probably see her as an outcast and treat her as such. However, it was her conviction that the God of the Hebrews would provide an absolute victory for the enemies of her people that propelled Rahab to accept the spies into her home, guaranteed the safety of her family, and placed her into the lineage of unequivocally the most important person to have ever lived, Jesus Christ (Matthew 1:5).

When I contemplate how God sees people, the way God sees me, I am beyond humbled. Despite all we do, just as the Pharisees of Matthew chapter 6 did, to appear good in the eyes of men and to be accepted by men, God is not fooled. He doesn't buy the front we put on nor the facade of the exterior. Having money and dressing in nice clothes doesn't draw us closer to God any more than being poor endears us to Him. He is not impressed with our lineage, nor is He repulsed by our lack of the "right" heritage (Acts 10:34). He genuinely looks inside of us and sees who we really are (1 Samuel 16:7). He is concerned with the disposition of our hearts, not with the positions we hold in the office, in the community, or even in the eyes of the rich and famous. He sees us—not who we profess to be or who others have projected us to be—and that humbles me.

It also comforts me because it tells me my past doesn't define who I am to God. I am as valuable to Him after I sinned as I was before I sinned. His love doesn't wain or fade depending upon if I'm accepted by man or rejected by man. To God, it isn't about looking right; it's about getting right with Him through obedience to the precious Gospel of Jesus Christ. It's about trusting Him with my "right now" as well as with my eternity. I am comforted because my soul is still worth something to God, no matter where I've been or what I've done. He demonstrated such in giving His only begotten Son, Jesus, to die on the cross for me when I was an ungodly sinner, who was without hope and stood as His enemy (Romans 5:6-8). Please don't be mistaken. It is not His will that any of us who have been clothed with Christ in baptism for the remission of our sins (Acts 2:38; Galatians

> To God, it isn't about looking right; it's about getting right with Him through obedience to the precious Gospel of Jesus Christ.

3:27) would continue in sin so that His grace would abound (Romans 6:1). However, when we do sin, He has provided the absolute best Advocate, Jesus Christ the righteous, to intercede on our behalf (1 John 2:1). Upon repentance, He receives us back into His fold (1 John 1:9). That's how God sees us, and He fully expects us to see others in the same way.

The Justified Man of James chapter 2 is the one who does just that. He understands that acceptable faith before God does not exist in the absence of the works that demonstrate that faith. In James 2:1, we read, "My brethren, do not hold your faith in our glorious Lord Jesus Christ with an attitude of personal favoritism."[4] As has been pointed out in the Learning section on chapter 2, the concept of personal favoritism means "to accept a face; to make unjust distinctions between people by treating one person better than another; to show favoritism, to be partial, partiality." In this case, the distinctions or judgments rendered are rooted in evil reasonings (2:4) that appear to be hoping for personal gain.

The Justified Man sees people differently. Instead of walking the path of partiality, he chooses to see the souls of men as valuable, regardless of their situation in life. This is because:

- James 2:1 - **The Justified Man Holds Faith with Proper Perspective**

    Being a follower of God, a true disciple, is not merely what the Justified Man does; it's who he is. Understanding that his salvation is anchored in the love that God has shown him through His Son, Jesus, this man leans into God in all areas of life. His standing in society is not part of the equation for how he sees others because this man clearly understands and accepts that faith in Jesus dictates the way he sees and treats others around him. Regardless of the religious practices or moral standards they currently adhere to, they are souls whom God loves and wants to redeem. The blood of Jesus was given, not for those who are already saved, but for those who need salvation. Thus, regardless of what kind of clothes they wear or how large their bank account is, the Justified Man sees them differently because he holds faith in our Lord Jesus Christ in proper perspective.

- James 2:4 - **The Justified Man Operates Without Evil Motives**

    Selfishness is a snare Satan loves to place before mankind. Our desire to look out for our interests is something we need to fight against. We see that brought to light in Philippians 2:4, when the Holy Spirit inspired the apostle Paul to write, "Do not merely look out for your own personal interests, but also for the interests of others." Before he wrote that, in verse 3, he penned, "Do nothing from selfishness or empty conceit." Selfishness stands in opposition to sacrifice and often drives the car of reasoning. Surrendering to Jesus in all facets of life places us solely as a passenger who goes where the driver of the car, God, would have us to go. This reality is why the Justified Man does not operate with evil motives. He has chosen to empty himself of seeking personal gain; he only wants gain for God. He has intentionally decided that seeking to glorify God in his life means he must treat his fellow man, all men, in a God-honoring manner. The Justified Man sets out to do just that.

- James 2:6 - **The Justified Man Knows God Alone Sits in the Place of Judge**

When we draw conclusions about people, we make determinations based upon what we can see. At times, the fruit in their life is clearly discernable (Matthew 7:15-20); however, with our inability to see into the heart of man (1 Samuel 16:7), we may misjudge and reach wrong conclusions. I firmly believe that's why the teaching of Jesus in Matthew 7:2, "For in the way you judge, you will be judged; and by your standard of measure, it will be measured to you," is in the text. We ought to always remember that there is one judge who presides in a courtroom. If there are multiple judges in the same room, chaos ensues. The Justified Man of James chapter 2 understands that there is one Judge, and God alone is to be that Judge (James 4:12). When it comes to genuinely seeing people, the Justified Man submits to God in areas of judgment.

2) LOVES PEOPLE THE WAY GOD LOVES PEOPLE - MERCIFULLY

If, however, you are fulfilling the royal law according to the Scripture, "You shall love your neighbor as yourself," you are doing well. (James 2:8)

It is impossible to discuss the Justified Man of James chapter 2 without a proper understanding of the royal law. Rooted in Leviticus 19:18, the royal law demands action. With James calling the saints to be effectual doers of the Word and not merely hearers (1:22-25), the imprint of discipleship is not merely in what information one has but is demonstrated in the tracks left behind in the deeds of obedience. It's not just about claiming we love God but showing we love Him. It's not merely claiming we love our neighbor; it's demonstrating this love in tangible, life-changing ways. This fundamental truth is the arch under which all others find substance. Love demands action, and that's why we need to consider how love and mercy are combined in chapter two, verses 8-13.

The word "love" used in verse 8 is agapáō and means "to esteem, love, indicating a direction of the will and finding one's joy in something or someone."[5] It differs from the love of philéō. Agape love is not a love of feeling or affection, and it is not expressed with a kiss or a hug. Instead, it is a love that desires what is best for another. It's a love of decision and directs the actions of the one loving, not necessarily of the one being loved. This form of love is not a reaction to the deeds of others. It's not love given because someone deserves it. Instead, it is love given before the other even loves in return. That's why, when we consider this kind of love, the standard that should rise above all is that of the love of God who loved us and determined to give His Son to die on the cross for us before any of mankind loved Him (1 John 4:19). Consider for a moment the way God loves us as outlined in 1 John chapter 4.

- 1 John 4:9 - **A Redeeming Love**

    "By this the love of God was manifested in us, that God has sent His only begotten Son into the world so that we might live through Him."

- 1 John 4:10 - **A Sacrificial Love**

    "In this is love, not that we loved God, but that He loved us and sent His Son to be the propitiation for our sins."

- 1 John 4:16 - **A Genuine Love**

    "We have come to know and have believed the love which God has for us. God is love, and the one who abides in love abides in God, and God abides in him."

- 1 John 4:19 - **An Initiating Love**

    "We love, because He first loved us."

This is only a tiny sampling of the verses describing God's love for mankind. A love of decision moves first, is authentic, sacrifices greatly, and demonstrates actions that seek the betterment of the one receiving the love. That's the same love we are called to have and to display in James chapter 2. It's the love our faith is rooted in as we contemplate our standing before God. Without the love of God, we have no hope and are doomed to hell. That's why, when we rest in the love of God that is saturated in His gracious mercy and yet do not give mercy to others, we sin. We cannot accept the gift of salvation from the One who gives all good things (James 1:17) without pouring forth mercy on our fellow man. It doesn't work that way. If we rest in the law of liberty, we are responsible to speak and act accordingly (James 1:25).

That's what the Justified Man does. He understands that faith is not merely hypothetical or theorized. Our faith demands practical application, necessitates fruitfulness, and requires effort. In our text, the action specifically being spoken of is extending mercy to others. Mercy is a word that means "compassion, active pity, with the sense of goodness in general."[6] It does not remove the responsibility of the guilty to turn from sinful ways in faithful obedience to the Gospel of Jesus Christ. Any mercy the Justified Man extends does not replace the need for the mercy of God in the life of the sinner. However, it does mean that the Justified Man will respond with kindness and compassion that is undeserved and rooted in love for one's neighbor

3) LIVES WITH AUTHENTICITY OF DISCIPLESHIP - OVERFLOW OF DEEDS

In Matthew 16:24, we read concerning being a disciple of Jesus Christ, "Then Jesus said to His disciples, 'If anyone wishes to come after Me, he must deny himself, and take up his cross and follow Me.'" In the entry for *disciple* in the *Encyclopedia of the Bible*, we learn that a disciple is "someone who follows another person or another way of life and who submits himself to the discipline (teaching) of that leader or way."[7] We see this concept on display when we think of individuals such as Peter, Andrew, James, and

John. These men left their way of life to pursue the Master, growing in their understanding of who He is, and putting what He taught into practice in their lives. When we contrast these imperfect but willing individuals in their pursuit of following Jesus with the wealthy man found in Matthew 19:16-22, a man who could not bring himself to surrender everything in his desire for eternal life, we see that being a disciple of Jesus means not holding anything back, even if it's for what we perceive as our security. When we look at the individuals in Luke 9:57-62 who made bold declarations to follow Jesus or were called by Jesus to follow Him, we learn that merely saying you want to follow Jesus is not the same as doing it. Faith demands action, and that's what the Justified Man of James 2 knows.

In James 2:14, two questions are posed to the audience.

- "What use is it, my brethren, if someone says he has faith but he has no works?"
- "Can that faith save him?"

The answer that follows is stated three times amidst the various illustrations.

- James 2:17 – "Even so faith, if it has no works is dead, being by itself."
- James 2:20 – "But are you willing to recognize, you foolish fellow, that faith without works is useless?"
- James 2:26 – "For just as the body without the spirit is dead, so also faith without works is dead."

A dead and useless faith cannot save. That's the point behind the illustration of the brother or sister in need (James 2:15-16). If all it takes is a mental acknowledgment that God is real and exists, then even the demons have a saving faith; however, that is not the case (James 2:19). Abraham demonstrated his faith when he took Isaac up the mountain to sacrifice him (Genesis 22). Rahab displayed great faith in God when she helped the messengers from the Hebrew people (Joshua 2). When we look deeper into Hebrews chapter 11, a consistent theme we observe in the lives of those listed is that by faith, they acted.

- v. 4 - Abel offered
- v. 7 - Noah prepared
- vv. 8,9 - Abraham obeyed and lived

- v. 11 - Sarah considered and conceived
- v. 17 - Abraham offered
- v. 20 - Isaac blessed
- v. 21 - Jacob blessed and worshiped
- v. 22 - Joseph gave orders
- v. 23 - The parents of Moses hid him
- v. 24 - Moses refused to be called the son of Pharaoh's daughter
- v. 25 - Moses chose to endure ill-treatment

The point is, their faith compelled them to act, and that's precisely what the Justified Man understands and does. His faith causes him to live authentically as a disciple of Jesus Christ. His faith is not merely lip service. He didn't check the boxes on the list and then sit down. The Justified Man expends himself in the service of the King because that's what being a disciple is all about. Faith demands it.

CONCLUSION

We began this chapter by asking a question regarding the existence of the laws of gravity and inertia, even if they are not visible or being tested and demonstrated in a laboratory. I asked that because a fundamental principle is applied in science when we are talking about laws of science and not merely theories. Theories are demonstratable sometimes. In contrast, laws have been tested repeatedly and have proved to be constant. I guess we could say that the laws of gravity and inertia are in the "law" category because they have passed the test. Even if no laboratory test is being conducted, the law of gravity exists and is constantly in effect. The same is true for the law of inertia. The significance of this point is that the laws themselves are so intertwined with the actions demanded by the laws that one cannot be valid without demonstrating such. They go together.

The same is true when we consider faith and works in James 2 in the life of the Justified Man. He's justified, or counted as righteous in the eyes of God, not because he has earned that status. Rather it is because he understands that God is the giver of salvation. The Justified Man has accepted that grace. When he obeyed the Gospel, it impacted his entire life. The works discussed in this chapter are not meritorious in nature; none are. However, they flow freely from the one who has genuine faith—looking at others as God does, loving others as God does, and living authentically as a disciple.

The challenge you and I have before us today is to honestly evaluate our walk with the Lord. Is our faith merely an intellectual concept? Do we approach faith from a selfish standpoint? Do we talk about many good works without ever engaging in them? Or are we, like the Justified Man, answering the demands of faith daily?

REFLECTION QUESTIONS

1. Since having genuine faith requires actions that reveal such, if people were looking at your life, what actions would they say point to your faith?
2. What does it mean to see people the way God sees people?
3. Why do some things get in your way of seeing people that way?
4. Reflecting on your own life, why is God's mercy so important to you?
5. Why is it essential for you to extend mercy to others?
6. What does it mean to live with authenticity in discipleship?

LESSONS FROM
THE WISE MAN

"Who among you is wise and understanding? Let him show by his good behavior his deeds in the gentleness of wisdom."

- James 3:13 -

INTRODUCTION

Usually, extreme examples are not great because they open to criticism the logical point trying to be made. However, extreme measures can also uniquely and forcefully drive home a point the writer or speaker attempts to communicate. With that in mind, I ask for you to bear with me as I begin this chapter with an extreme illustration and then narrow our thoughts to a practical application.

Imagine yourself waking up early in the morning before the sun is above the horizon. It's still very dark outside. Inside the house, the darkness looms like a dense fog. You don't want to awaken your spouse, so you shuffle to the bathroom where your robe is hanging. You brush your teeth and ready yourself to go downstairs, make coffee, and enjoy your morning quiet time of Bible reading and catching up on the news. As you quietly leave the bedroom, you close the door behind you. With a sense of freedom from the constraints of a sleeping spouse, you reach over to turn on the light in the hallway only to hear a car horn begin to blast outside. You rush over to the window to look down on your vehicles. It's your car that is sounding its horn. But why? You don't have the facts; however, you also do not wish to be known as "that neighbor" who wakes everyone up.

As you rush down the stairs on your way to turning off the horn, you flip the switch at the bottom of the stairs to turn off the light to the hallway. Suddenly, you notice the car horn stops. That's odd, you think to yourself, so you go outside to double-check the door. The car is locked just like you left it the night before. There are no signs of forced entry or any sort of burglary, so you go back inside thinking it must have been a fluke.

As the smell of freshly brewed coffee begins to waft through the house, you remember you forgot something upstairs in the bedroom. Just before quietly making your way up the stairs, you flip the light switch to illuminate the way. The lights come on—and so does the horn to the car. "What is going on?" you mutter under your breath. You switch off the light to the hallway as you turn to go back outside. The car horn turns off.

An idea pops into your head. Why is it that when I turn the light switch off, the car alarm turns off. Why does the car horn begin to sound when I turn the light switch on? Your curiosity gets the best of you, so you walk back over to the light switch and turn it back on. As sure as the morning is beginning to slip away, the car horn blasts again. When you flip the switch off, the horn stops. That's weird, you think to yourself as you try it a few more times.

"Why would the light switch turn on the car horn?"

Both operate by electricity; however, the light switch should not influence the car horn. It is not sensible, that's not how electricity works, it's not right, and it ought not to be.

Extreme, I know.

Who's ever heard of a light switch that is not connected to a car horn providing the completion of an electrical circuit to that horn? It's not reasonable, and it would never happen because there are laws to electricity. While electricity can jump from one line to another, it's unheard of for this to happen when it comes to a light switch and a car horn.

Just as this example is absurd, James, in chapter 3, points the readers to illustrations that are just as illogical when teaching how those claiming to be wise teachers are using their tongues to bless God while turning around and cursing others.

> *With it we bless our Lord and Father, and with it we curse men, who have been made in the likeness of God; from the same mouth come both blessing and cursing. My brethren, these things ought not to be this way.* (James 3:9-10)

This behavior is entirely foreign to the person walking with wisdom from above and practicing the Royal Law. That's why James takes the time to pause and discuss the tongue in further detail. He had already raised the subject when dealing with how they spoke toward God when tempted (1:13) and how they dishonored God and man when they showed personal favoritism in the synagogue (2:1, 3). Apparently, consistency and authenticity are a real struggle for these early Christians, and they need to continually be transformed in the renewing of their mind (Rom. 12:2). However, a Wise Man stands out in this chapter, and it's this man we want to learn from and begin to mimic in our own lives.

THE WISE MAN...

1) DEVOTES TIME PREPARING HIMSELF TO TEACH GOD'S WORD

Time is a currency that can only be spent once. Like money has great purchasing power, time should be viewed similarly. Only with time, there are no refunds. With the purchase made with money, if you don't like it or it doesn't fit, usually you can take it back to the store. Time doesn't work that way. Once you spend it, it's gone. That's why what David wrote in Psalm 39:4-5 is so true and significant.

Time is a currency that can only be spent once.

> *Lord, make me to know my end*
>
> *And what is the extent of my days;*
>
> *Let me know how transient I am.*
>
> *Behold, You have made my days as handbreadths,*
>
> *And my lifetime as nothing in Your sight;*
>
> *Surely every man at his best is a mere breath.*

That's also why what we find here in James chapter 4, verse 14 is worthy of being prioritized in our minds, "You are just a vapor that appears for a little while and then vanishes away." Not only is your life short on this earth and short in the grand scheme of eternity, but your time on this side of eternity is also limited. David prays that God will allow him to know and remember this fact. The implication is that knowing he is transient here in this life will inspire him to use what little time he has well.

With that in mind, I would like you to think about a concept regarding the use of our time in this earthly life. Think for a moment about an athlete who competes at the highest level possible in their particular sport, much like an Olympic athlete or a Major League baseball player. Did that person wake up one day and, on a whim, decide she was going to play at that level? She has never played the sport in her life; however, as the sun rises one day, she thinks to herself, I believe today I will suit up for the Olympics and go compete in the next games. Or he thinks, I know I've never played baseball, but I am ready to go play for the Atlanta Braves. Does anybody really think that way?

The apparent conclusion is absolutely not!

The people who compete at such high levels have spent a lifetime preparing themselves. From the time they were children, they have displayed intense levels of dedication and sacrifice. Their workout routine, sleep regiment, nutrition guidelines, mental study times, and hours upon hours of practice have gotten them to a point where their skill set is ready to be put to the test against the best in their sport. When the other kids played video games, they were most likely in the gym. When their peers were sleeping in on a Saturday morning after staying out late on Friday, the athletes who compete at high levels were most likely up and running mile after mile. When friends practiced little or no self-control in what they ate, these athletes refused to put foods into their bodies that would not be the most beneficial fuels to keep them excelling. In other words, an athlete doesn't reach this caliber by accident. A significant level of self-control must be present (1 Cor. 9:25).

In the same way, but in a field that has a far more significant impact than sports ever could, a teacher of God's Word should not wake up one day, without serious dedication, preparation, and supplication, and decide to teach and preach God's Word. This is the point Paul makes as he writes to a younger evangelist, Timothy, "Be diligent to present yourself approved to

God a workman who does not need to be ashamed, accurately handling the word of truth" (2 Tim. 2:15). Here, the phrase "be diligent" means "to make every effort to do one's best, to be eager."[1] The English definition of "eager" is "marked by enthusiastic or impatient desire or interest."[2] In other words, Paul is telling Timothy that in order to present himself before God as one who handles the Word of Truth accurately, he must, with enthusiasm and impatient desire, give his absolute best effort in studying the Truth. Then he will be able to not only teach the Truth of God's Word to the people in Ephesus, he will be equipped with the knowledge to live God's Word before them as an example of righteousness.

With this in mind, let's return to James chapter 3. The warning found in verses 1-2 is significant; however, Paul is not trying to deter those who would like to teach God's Word from doing so. After all, all Christians are responsible for teaching as we make disciples (Matt. 28:19-20). Rather, he is putting into perspective the reality that teachers will be held accountable for how they walk as disciples of Jesus Christ and for what they teach. In doing so, he refers to a "stricter judgment" that will fall upon teachers. As ones who can influence others with the words they speak and the conclusions they reach, teachers, with great enthusiasm and an impatient desire to know the truth of God's Word, better spend the currency of their time in delving into the Word of God for themselves. Proclamation before preparation should be prohibited. The Wise Man of James chapter 3 knows and follows this.

2) PRAYERFULLY SEEKS GOD'S BLESSING WITHOUT SEEKING GOD'S CURSING ON OTHERS

Why would someone seek the downfall of another person? Why would he seek for harm to befall another? While the answers to these questions and others along the same lines could be vast and plentiful, the real question is, "Is there ever a good reason to ask for God to harm another who is made in His image?"

Do you remember the teaching of Jesus about forgiveness in Matthew 18? In that passage, Peter asked, "Lord, how often shall my brother sin against me and I forgive him? Up to seven times?" (v. 21). Jesus responded, "I do not say to you up to seven times, but up to seventy times seven" (v. 22). You'll remember that Jesus then illustrated this point by telling a parable about a king who wished to settle his accounts with his servants. One of the slaves owed the king 10,000 talents. This would be in the billions of dollars by today's standards. The servant did not have the means to repay this enormous debt, so the king called for him to be sold, along with his entire family. With great desperation, the slave fell to the ground and begged for mercy, saying, "Have patience with me and I will repay you everything" (v. 26). The Bible says that the lord of that slave felt "compassion and released him and forgave him the debt" (v. 27).

As Jesus continued the parable, He introduced another individual who was indebted to the slave who had been forgiven. Only in this interaction, mercy was not extended. Instead, the forgiven slave went out seeking the one who owed him money. The amount was not comparable, only a hundred denarii or roughly five months' worth of wages. Jesus said the forgiven slave "seized him and began to choke him, saying, 'Pay back what you owe'" (v. 28). This slave, just like the original slave, fell to the ground and begged for mercy. However, in this scenario, there was no mercy given. The second slave was thrown in prison until he could pay back everything he owed to the first slave.

Of all the interesting details in this parable, one that stands out to me is the impact this had on those who saw the interaction. Jesus says that "when his fellow slaves saw what had happened, they were deeply grieved and came and reported to their lord all that had happened" (v. 31). We must never forget that our actions and attitudes are constantly being observed, and bystanders will draw conclusions about us and the God we serve based upon what they see. What these individuals witnessed impacted them to the point of being "deeply grieved." Therefore, they were moved to action to remedy the wrong they perceived.

> *We must never forget that our actions and attitudes are constantly being observed, and bystanders will draw conclusions about us and the God we serve based upon what they see.*

Jesus concluded this parable with the original slave being brought back before the king and held accountable. The servant, who had at one time experienced the forgiveness of the king, lost his comfort and freedom because he refused to extend mercy to another who was indebted to him. Jesus ended this parable by telling Peter and any others who had gathered, "My heavenly Father will also do the same to you, if each of you does not forgive his brother from your heart" (v. 35).

The impact of Jesus' teaching on this subject in Matthew 18 has far-reaching implications. With God's blessings extended to us because of our relationship with Him through the blood of His Son, Jesus Christ, we are to be a changed people. We are to:

- "walk no longer as the Gentiles walk" (Eph. 4:17)
- "walk in love, just as Christ also loved you" (Eph. 5:2)
- "walk as children of Light" (Eph. 5:8)
- "walk, not as unwise men but as wise" (Eph. 5:15)

This applies to the Christians James is writing to as well. When they accept the grace of God in the forgiveness He offers through Jesus, they are to be a transformed (Rom. 12:2) and renewed (Eph. 4:23) people. The behavior described in James 3 regarding the tongue that "directs the entire body" (v. 3), "defiles the entire body" (v. 6), and is full of "deadly poison" (v. 8) is not the picture of a transformed and renewed people. Teachers who ask for God's blessing on themselves, with full expectation God will provide, while asking for God to curse others who are made in His image is not what God desires. To emphasize this point, the apostle Paul turns to nature as he writes regarding the tongue,

> *With it we bless our Lord and Father, and with it we curse men, who have been made in the likeness of God; from the same mouth come both blessing and cursing. My brethren, these things ought not to be this way. Does a fountain send out from the same opening both fresh and bitter water? Can a fig tree, my brethren, produce olives, or a vine produce figs? Nor can salt water produce fresh.* (vv. 9-12)

The Wise Man of James chapter 3 is consistent with what he teaches and what he asks of God for himself. It's not that he's perfect in all he does (James 3:8); however, he has made a conscious decision, backed with tremendous effort, to live consistently before God and others. When he fails, he seeks forgiveness. When others seek his harm, he looks to Jesus' example when He was being nailed to the cross and asked His Father to "forgive them; for they do not know what they are doing" (Luke 23:34). The Wise Man of James 3

> The Wise Man of James 3 refuses to ask God to rain down His cursing upon his enemies.

refuses to ask God to rain down His cursing upon his enemies.

3) PRODUCES FRUIT CONSISTENT WITH HEAVENLY WISDOM

When you bite into an apple, you expect to taste the apple. If you ever bit into an apple and tasted anything but an apple, you would be shocked and surprised. That's because it's logical and reasonable to draw conclusions based upon what you observe. Our minds tend to work that way, which can either be a great blessing or a great hindrance when it comes to our influence. That's because people will draw conclusions about us based upon what we say and what we do. If we profess to be Christians but do not act in ways that demonstrate such a claim, they will conclude that we aren't very serious about our faith or that we don't believe what we are teaching.

In the same way, if we declare to be disciples of Jesus Christ, and by the actions in our lives, we demonstrate such to be the case, people who observe us will generate conclusions about us based upon their observations. They will think that we are serious about our faith and that we fully believe what we are teaching. That is because our brains are wired to process what we hear through the filters of what we observe. If there is a lack of consistency, confusion results and conclusions will reflect this.

This inconsistency is written about time and time again in the pages of God's Word. Consider the following verses:

- "Then Jesus spoke to the crowds and to His disciples, saying: 'The scribes and the Pharisees have seated themselves in the chair of Moses; therefore all that they tell you, do and observe, but do not do according to their deeds; for they say *things* and do not do *them*'" (Matt. 23:1-3).
- "Therefore you have no excuse, everyone of you who passes judgment, for in that which you judge another, you condemn yourself; for you who judge practice the same things. And we know that the judgment of God rightly falls upon those who practice such things. But do you suppose this, O man, when you

pass judgment on those who practice such things and do the same *yourself*, that you will escape the judgment of God?" (Rom. 2:1-3)

When people act in ways that are not consistent with what they claim, it is called hypocrisy. This word is found one time in the book of James, and it's right here in our chapter under consideration (3:17). It means "to pretend, simulate."[3] In our text, we are told that the Wise Man conducts his life and teaching without hypocrisy, meaning he does not profess one thing and act in a way inconsistent with what he says. He is unlike the scribes and Pharisees whom Jesus reprimanded in Matthew 23 by saying, "Woe to you, scribes and Pharisees, hypocrites! For you clean the outside of the cup and of the dish, but inside they are full of robbery and self-indulgence. You blind Pharisee, first clean the inside of the cup and of the dish, so that the outside of it may become clean also" (vv.25-26). The Wise Man of James 3 operates with wisdom from above (3:17) instead of the wisdom of an earthly, natural, and demonic nature (3:15).

In verses 13-18 of chapter 3, James illuminates the stark contrast between the two. Verse 13 serves as the base upon which the rest of the house is built: "Who among you is wise and understanding? Let him show by his good behavior his deeds in the gentleness of wisdom" (3:13). James is telling them to prove it. If they consider themselves to have the knowledge and ability to teach, and they apply such knowledge, then the deeds they display should be evidence of such. However, in going back to 3:1, we understand some wanted to be teachers who may have the correct information, but they are void of the demonstration of such information in their own lives. Therefore, intellectually, they believe they are operating according to the wisdom that is from above; however, in practicality, they need this warning from James. If jealousy and selfish ambition are the motives driving their activities, they are in fact operating with the wisdom that is not from above.

The Wise Man of James 3 can discern this. He does not merely understand the facts of what he is teaching and how he is living, but he can effectively investigate the motivation of his heart and guard against self-seeking and self-elevating desires. How does he do that? He understands the seed must be planted if it's ever going to grow and produce fruit after its kind. It seems that some of those to whom James is writing understand the importance of the seed; however, in their own lives, they have yet to allow the seed to be planted and watered so it can grow accordingly.

CONCLUSION

Since becoming a youth and family minister in 2000, I have found the study of the teenage mind an exciting one. As people mature from the simple joys of childhood and advance into the more grown-up concepts of adulthood, this no-man's-land between known as adolescence is steeped in significant changes. Some include changes in the way they dress, the hobbies they enjoy, and even the music they prefer. The rapid physical changes are only matched by the social tide that seems to change by the moment. One of the most significant changes in teenagers' minds is the belief that they know more than they know. While it's true that they have grown intellectually through the years, their ability to put that knowledge into practical application in their lives is not always there due to the lack of development in the prefrontal cortex of their brains.

The human brain's prefrontal cortex doesn't fully develop until the age of 25.[4] This portion of the brain serves as the connection between reason and action. That's why there are times we adults struggle to understand why teenagers do things that seem to be inconsistent with their knowledge. While they are still responsible and accountable for the wrongs they commit, we should be aware that sometimes the wiring of this portion of their brains may not be complete. The truth is, for teenagers, it's not supposed to be there until they mature and develop beyond the years of adolescence. Therefore, as adults who may influence their lives, we have to help them connect the dots and apply the knowledge they do have to daily life.

Maturity is a huge factor in the text we are examining. As we continue to grow, we often realize just how much we don't know and how immature our motivations can be. We are faced with the realities of our inadequacies, which will either cause us to embrace continued learning or will cause us to become stuck in the rut of our lack of understanding. The Christians to whom James is writing appear to be either in such a rut or in danger of becoming so. The actions and motivations he warns against are what we would assume either a very young, immature Christian might become entangled in or are consistent with the inconsistency of hypocrisy. Like the light switch that controlled the car horn in the introduction, the fallacy of the "Christian" hypocrite is crystal clear in this chapter. He is one who teaches without timely preparation, who seeks God's blessing in his own life while asking God to curse other people, and who claims to be wise but is motivated by earthly wisdom saturated in jealously and selfish ambition.

The Wise Man is not wise by his own doing. Instead, he is considered wise because the seed sown in his life, the Word of Truth (3:14), has been allowed to germinate and blossom. The fruit he displays is that which is considered "righteousness" or a demonstration that he has conformed to the claims of a higher authority and stands in opposition to lawlessness.[5] As the seed continues to grow and the fruit continues to mature, so the Wise Man continues to grow in purity, peace, gentleness, reasonableness, mercy, and dedicated consistency in his walk.

REFLECTION QUESTIONS

1. Since studying God's Word is crucial to your maturing in the faith, how much time a day do you spend in this area? What are the most significant obstacles in your day to spending more time devoted to studying God's Word? In what ways could you improve this aspect of your life?

2. Do you find it difficult to pray to God on behalf of those who have hurt you or are challenging to be around? If so, why do you think that is?

3. Since others are constantly viewing our actions, what do your actions reveal about 1) God and 2) you as a disciple of Jesus Christ?

4. In what ways do you wish you could be more consistent with what the Bible teaches?

LESSONS FROM
THE HUMBLE MAN

"Humble yourselves in the presence of the Lord, and He will exalt you."

- James 4:10 -

INTRODUCTION

First published in 1886 by Scottish author Robert Louis Stevenson, the "penny dreadful" known as *The Strange Case of Dr. Jekyll and Mr. Hyde* has become known as one of the most fantastic allegories of all time. Perhaps it's because humanity has been and remains enthralled with the turmoil that exists within us as our desires battle between good and evil. Or, perhaps it's simply because the book was so well written that Robert Louis Stevenson, who was sick in bed while writing it, is forever regarded as one of the greatest writers of all time. For whatever reason, *The Strange Case of Dr. Jekyll and Mr. Hyde* is still required reading for most students of the English language and British literature.

As the plot unfolds, the main characters, Doctor Henry Jekyll and Edward Hyde, are intricately connected, as you know, being the same physical person. The serum that separates them holds the power between the good of Dr. Jekyll and the evil of Mr. Hyde. At the beginning of the story, Dr. Jekyll controls this transition as he decides when to ingest it. However, with every wavering transition, the serum seems to take more and more control. Thus, toward the end of the novel, Dr. Jekyll locks himself in his laboratory in fear of what will happen; for Mr. Hyde is no longer invited into his life but has assumed residency at will. In the end, the only thing that will stop Mr.

Hyde's evil excursions is death, which ultimately is how Stevenson's literary masterpiece ends.

While *The Strange Case of Dr. Jekyll and Mr. Hyde* has been analyzed in just about every possible way known to man, from human psychology to literary pieces, our interest is focused on the rivalry that lies within the main character. Dr. Jekyll brings forth Mr. Hyde as a way to pseudo-consciously allow for the expression of unrestrained evil. The more collected and supposedly moral doctor must then battle with the regret and remorse which follows each horrendous death. This continual vacillation between the two manifestations of Dr. Jekyll is tortuous. For our consideration in this lesson, it stands as a dark illustration of how horrible life can be when one waivers between unrestrained, selfish lusts and the submissive walk of a disciple of Jesus Christ.

In James chapter 4, we see two character traits, two pathways shall we say, as rivals. The first is pride and the second is humility. We will learn more about the Humble Man of this chapter in the Discussion portion. For the time being, I would like us to discover what the pathway of pride looks like and what are the results that follow. To draw the audience closer to the Humble Man, James emphasizes what humility is not in order to paint the true picture of what humility is.

As chapter 4 begins, James confronts these Christians on some of the "fruit" in their lives. Let us take special note of what these fruits are and why they exist.

- 4:1 – "quarrels"
- 4:1 – "conflicts"
    - The source of both is their "pleasures" that wage an internal war at the seat of their desires and passions.
    - The word "pleasures" means "physical pleasure" and often refers to sensual pleasure, desire, appetite, or lust.[1]
- 4:2 – "do not have"
    - The precursor is that they "lust," meaning "to have the affections directed toward something, to lust, desire, long after; in a bad sense of coveting and lusting after."[2]
    - As a result of this, they commit murder.

- 4:2 – "cannot obtain"
    - The description before this result is that they are "envious," meaning "to be zealous, filled with zeal, zealously affected."[3]
    - As a result, they quarrel, seeking their interests and desires.
- 4:2 – "do not have"
    - We see that they are empty once again; however, the reason given here is that they do not humble themselves to the point of petitioning God.
- 4:3 – "do not receive"
    - Here their fruit comes full circle; these Christians do not receive what they ask for because their only motive is to indulge in their pleasures.

Consider these actions and results. They are a pleasure-seeking, lust-driven, destruction-fabricating, envy-saturated people who are constantly fighting within themselves and with others in the body of Christ as they jockey for significance and prominence. They receive nothing from God because they are not seeking His interest but merely their own. As a result of this, James calls them "adulteresses." At this remark, the spiritual adultery of Israel in the Old Testament surfaces in the minds of serious Bible students. These individuals who come from the covenant people of God, as identified in James 1:1, are being severely scorned as they are warned about friendship with the world and the subsequent hostility with God that is the result. All of this is because they are self-seeking and not submissive to God. That's what the proud pathway looks like in James chapter 4.

As the serious Bible student combs through the pages of Scripture, he will be hard pressed to find a positive statement about this pathway. Repeatedly, God warns against the path of pride and promises the end of this journey will be dishonor and destruction. Thus, the rival pathway of the humble is shown to be pride—the rival whose end is dishonor and punishment; whereas the humble will attain wisdom. Consider the following:

> *Repeatedly, God warns against the path of pride and promises the end of this journey will be dishonor and destruction.*

- "The Lord will tear down the house

of the **proud**, But He will establish the boundary of the widow" (Prov. 15:25).
- "Everyone who is **proud** in heart is an abomination to the Lord; Assuredly, he will not be unpunished" (Prov. 16:5).
- "Haughty eyes and a **proud** heart, the lamp of the wicked, is sin" (Prov. 21:4).
- "For the Lord of hosts will have a day of reckoning against everyone who is **proud** and lofty and against everyone who is lifted up, that he may be abased" (Isa. 2:12).
- "**Pride** goes before destruction, and a haughty spirit before stumbling" (Prov. 16:18).
- "When **pride** comes, then comes dishonor, but with the humble is wisdom" (Prov. 11:2).

In chapter 4, we witness the Humble Man. Just as Dr. Jekyll and Mr. Hyde are rivals within one man, pride and humility seem to contend within the Christians in James' audience. Chances are, at least for some of us, we too struggle with this same rivalry. The task now is to investigate the Humble Man and glean from him what we may. We want to see him, not only for what he is not but also for who and what he is.

THE HUMBLE MAN...

1) SUBMITS TO GOD

The concept of submission is literally "to place in order. To place under in an orderly fashion."[4] It carries a military idea of a lower-ranking individual choosing to place himself under the authority of a higher-ranking individual. Perhaps the simplest way of thinking of this concept is as freely giving up oneself and one's way to another. Like a soldier who does what his superior officer commands or an employee who doesn't pursue her agenda but rather the direction her boss sets forth, the Christian is called to freely and willingly surrender his life to the will of God. Jesus made this point clear. In describing what it means to be a disciple of His, He said, "If anyone wishes to come after Me, he must deny himself, and take up his cross and follow

Me" (Matt. 16:24). To truly drive home the point of how much submission entails, Jesus continued saying, "For whoever wishes to save his life will lose it; but whoever loses his life for My sake will find it" (Matt. 16:25). In both statements, Jesus succinctly reveals that partial submission does not exist. The idea of such is foreign to the very definition of the term. Therefore, submitting to God is a total "all in or not in at all" reality.

The most remarkable example of what submission looks like in real life is seen in the last days of Jesus before His crucifixion. As He was facing the humiliation of the cross, Jesus prayed in the Garden of Gethsemane, "My Father, if it is possible, let this cup pass from Me; yet not as I will, but as You will" (Matt. 26:39). As the crossroads of Christ being fully human and yet fully God intersected, Jesus "humbled Himself by becoming obedient to the point of death, even death on a cross" (Phil. 2:8). There has never been, and there will never be, a more significant example of what it means to submit one's will to another.

Bringing oneself under control to the point of being able to freely and willingly submit to another means that you must turn from attitudes, behaviors, and beliefs that act opposed to submission. Having a child who does what his parents tell him to do with grumbling and complaining is not the same as having a child willingly submitting to his parents. Behavior can be demanded and obedience rendered to such; however, submission includes so much more than merely one's actions.

> *Bringing oneself under control to the point of being able to freely and willingly submit to another means that you must turn from attitudes, behaviors, and beliefs that act opposed to submission.*

In our text, James explains that to submit to God, one must be actively resisting the devil and actively drawing near to God. It's the concept of saying no to the bad and yes to the good; or it's like turning away from the wrong direction so you can purposely go in the right direction. These activities happen simultaneously; therefore, you cannot do one without the other happening as well. That's why to submit to God, the Humble Man teaches us that he is willing to aggressively say no to the devil and yes to God.

2) MAINTAINS A PROPER PERSPECTIVE OF HIS SIN

Have you seen those images where you are challenged to look for smaller pictures hidden within? Some find this an easy task because they are accustomed to rotating the image and seeing it from multiple directions, forcing them to see it from a different perspective. Others get very frustrated with this exercise because no matter how hard they try, their mind struggles to see the image as anything other than what they initially concluded the image to be. The perspective they settle on can actually be a hindrance in this case.

Perspective is an interesting filter that is shaped by culture, experience, morals, and family upbringing. If your filter has been set to process certain topics or events in a particular way, it's challenging to understand the scenario in an alternative way. If we are going to grow and change our perspectives, there must be a change in thinking and focus throughout our daily lives. There may be an abandonment of the teachings we received when we were young, and thus an internal struggle will exist. It's not as easy as snapping one's fingers and deciding things will be different immediately. You don't go to bed one night and wake up the following day with a changed way of filtering life's events. Often, a change in perspective takes time. Maturation must take place, and when it does, it's like a new light has been turned on in our minds. We are forever changed as this new filter serves as our fresh perspective.

When we look to the Humble Man of James chapter 4, we see a man who maintains a proper perspective of his sin and the severity of such. The cleansing of his deeds and the purifying of his heart are present because he wants to be pleasing to God. However, just like obedience can be forced in a child/parent relationship, people can convince themselves they are doing what God wants simply because they aren't doing "bad things."

In this chapter, James explains that sin should profoundly impact our lives. The commands to "be miserable," "mourn," "weep," and "let your laughter be turned into mourning" might seem odd to us. However, he is forcefully driving home the point that when one sees the sin in his life through its impact on his relationship with God, it ought to hurt. It's not a time for laughing and light-heartedly continuing in life. Instead, it's a pivotal moment. It's a time to feel the weight. It is vital to understand what sin is and what it does, so we will appropriately appreciate the greatness of what God has done for us through His Son.

- "Everyone who practices sin also practices lawlessness; and sin is lawlessness" (1 John 3:4).
- "The one who practices sin is of the devil; for the devil has sinned from the beginning" (1 John 3:8).
- "For the wages of sin is death" (Rom. 6:23).
- "But encourage one another day after day, as long as it is still called 'Today,' so that none of you will be hardened by the deceitfulness of sin" (Heb. 3:13).
- "But your iniquities have made a separation between you and your God, And your sins have hidden His face from you so that He does not hear" (Isa. 59:2).

When I think of keeping the proper perspective of sin in our lives, I am reminded of the parable of the Pharisee and the publican in Luke chapter 18. In this, Jesus tells of a self-righteous individual, the Pharisee, who genuinely believed he was pleasing to God almost more because of what he didn't do than what he did. Standing and praying to himself, this individual said, "God, I thank You that I am not like other people: swindlers, unjust, adulterers, or even like this tax collector. I fast twice a week; I pay tithes of all that I get" (Luke 18:11-12). By contrast, the publican, or tax collector, couldn't even look up. He simply prayed, "God, be merciful to me, the sinner!" (18:13) It's evident that one of these individuals, the tax collector, truly understood the weight and severity of his own sin.

The good news of the Gospel of Jesus Christ is that our past sins do not have to define our future.

We should not move beyond this section without saying that the good news of the Gospel of Jesus Christ is that our past sins do not have to define our future. In Christ, we find forgiveness and redemption (Eph. 1). Our sins are forgiven through obedience to the Gospel (Acts 2:38), and we are raised to walk in newness of life (2 Cor. 5:14-21). The fantastic news of the Gospel means that we have hope rooted in the iron-clad promises of God. However, that doesn't mean that we don't need to be reminded of where we would be if it weren't for the free gift of God in Christ Jesus (Rom. 6:23). The Humble Man of James chapter 4 remembers this and maintains a proper perspective of sin, what it did in his life, and what God has done through Jesus.

3) HUMBLES HIMSELF AND DOESN'T WAIT TO BE HUMBLED

Humbling can occur in multiple ways. A football team that is favored to win the big game can be humbled by the underdog who shows that, on any given night, anyone can win. The straight-A student who believes she is going to ace the test without studying can be humbled when she receives her paper back with a C- written on the top; she realizes that she must still work at getting good grades. The employee who believes he will get the promotion is humbled when he finds out that he was passed over for another candidate. These and countless other illustrations serve as a reminder that humbling isn't always one's own idea.

In Luke 14: 7-11, Jesus illustrates this concept when talking to the invited guests at the dinner of a prominent Pharisee. He noticed they were each trying to position themselves to be as close to the head of the table as possible. That makes sense in most settings because wherever the head of the table is, that's where the most important person in the room will be. The head of the table is also desired because that's where the day's business will be discussed. For those trying to position themselves, the embarrassment comes when a person of a higher rank enters the room. According to custom, if a person who outranked you entered the room to sit at the table, you would be asked to move down away from the head. That's why Jesus tells them that it's better for them to sit further down the table and be asked to move up rather than sit too close to the head and be told to move down. In one case, we see what self-humbling looks like; in the other, we see imposed humbling.

The Humble Man of James 4 doesn't wait around to be humbled. He willingly humbles himself before the Lord. It's a conscious decision and one that impacts every area of his life—his marriage, his parenting, his employment, his entertainment, his morality. Every facet of his life is brought under the authority of God as he gladly accepts that his life is hidden in Christ. He seeks to glorify the One who made his escape from sin possible by His own sacrifice (Gal. 2:20).

This concept is not rare in the Bible. As a matter of fact, we see the importance of humbling oneself in both the Old Testament and the New.

- "If I shut up the heavens so that there is no rain, or if I command the locust to devour the land, or if I send pestilence among My people, and My people who are called by My name humble themselves and pray and seek My face and turn from their wicked ways, then I will hear from heaven, will forgive their sin and will heal their land" (2 Chron. 7:13-14).
- "On exactly the tenth day of this seventh month is the day of atonement; it shall be a holy convocation for you, and you shall humble your souls and present an offering by fire to the Lord" (Lev. 23:27).
- "'Because your heart was tender and you humbled yourself before the Lord when you heard what I spoke against this place and against its inhabitants that they should become a desolation and a curse, and you have torn your clothes and wept before Me, I truly have heard you,' declares the Lord" (2 Kings 22:19).
- "To sum up, all of you be harmonious, sympathetic, brotherly, kindhearted, and humble in spirit" (1 Peter 3:8).
- "Therefore, humble yourselves under the mighty hand of God, that He may exalt you at the proper time" (1 Peter 5:6).

> *The Humble Man of James 4 doesn't wait around to be humbled. He willingly humbles himself before the Lord.*

The reality is that all of us will be humbled, either on this side of eternity or the other. There will be a time when every knee will bow before God, and every tongue will praise God (Rom. 14:11). The Humble Man of James chapter 4 has decided to do this now. As a result, God promises the forgiveness of his sins and an eternity in heaven.

CONCLUSION

There have been some great rivals in the history of humanity. Ali and Frazier, the Yankees and Red Sox, and even Batman and Joker all stand out.

However, none compare to the rivalry that exists between good and evil. As we reflect on James chapter 4 and the lessons learned from the Humble Man, we can't help but look in the mirror of our own lives. We are forced to answer the question, which path am I on, that of pride or humility? We are reminded that there is no partial submission to God and that being humble is something we aren't to wait on others, or on circumstances, to accomplish in our lives. If we are going to be exalted by God, we must initiate this in our lives and choose humility.

We'll end this lesson on humility with a story to consider.

Shortly after Booker T. Washington took over the presidency of Tuskegee Institute in Alabama in 1881, a story recounts a time when he was walking in an exclusive section of town. A wealthy white woman stopped him. Not knowing the famous Mr. Washington by sight, she asked if he would like to earn a few dollars by chopping wood for her. Because he had no pressing business at the moment, Professor Washington smiled, rolled up his sleeves, and proceeded to do the humble chore she had requested. When he was finished, he carried the logs into the house and stacked them by the fireplace. A little girl recognized him and later revealed his identity to the lady.

The next morning the embarrassed woman went to see Mr. Washington in his office at the Institute and apologized profusely. "It's perfectly all right, Madam," he replied. "Occasionally, I enjoy a little manual labor. Besides, it's always a delight to do something for a friend." She shook his hand warmly and assured him that his meek and gracious attitude had endeared him and his work to her heart. Not long afterward, she showed her admiration by persuading some wealthy acquaintances to join her in donating thousands of dollars to the Tuskegee Institute.[5]

If we want the reward God promises in eternity, we must make that clear now. James chapter 4 clarifies that it begins and ends with us humbling ourselves before God, no longer seeking after our own pleasures, lusts, and ways. That's what the Humble Man teaches us.

REFLECTION QUESTIONS

1. What is the biggest reason you might find yourself wavering

between selfish lusts of the flesh and the submissive walk of a disciple of Jesus Christ?

2. How has your past shaped your perspective of sin? Your culture, experiences, morals, and family upbringing?

3. What are some reasons that some people convince themselves they are doing what God wants them to do by merely not doing "bad things?"

4. Why is it a better idea to humble oneself rather than to be humbled by others? What does it say about that man who can humble himself?

LESSONS FROM
THE PATIENT MAN

"You too be patient; strengthen your hearts, for the coming of the Lord is near."

- James 5:8 -

INTRODUCTION

As a way of introducing this lesson, let's play a mental game. I will give you a couple of scenarios, and you think about the central struggle in each.

Scenario One: One summer day in July, a young boy found himself playing at his grandparents' house. He loved coming over to Grandma and Grandpa's house because he enjoyed interacting with them, and he was drawn to the way they smiled at him and wanted to be with him. However, perhaps the thing he looked forward to the most was how Grandma would cook treats for him. On this day, it was no different.

As he and Grandma stood in the kitchen, she began getting all the ingredients together to make homemade chocolate chip cookies. He loved baking with his grandma, so he was overjoyed when she asked him to help. Together, they made the batter, added the chocolate chips, placed the pieces of batter on cookie sheets, and put them into the oven. As they baked, the aroma created was so sweet to him. Grandma told him it would take about 12 minutes before they could get the first batch of cookies out of the oven, so he was free to play. The problem was that the longer they baked, the better they looked as he gazed at them through the little window in the oven door. The smell of the baking cookies wafted throughout the house, drawing his mother and grandfather to the source of deliciousness.

When the timer sounded, he began to salivate because he knew that meant it was time to remove them from the oven. He couldn't wait to taste them, so as soon as his grandmother took them out of the oven, he reached for one. His grandmother abruptly stop him. "You'll burn yourself, honey!" she lovingly exclaimed. "We'll need to let them cool first."

Disappointed, he saw her put them on the cooling rack. Seeing and smelling the freshly baked cookies was almost too much. He tried to go into the other room so that he wouldn't think about them, but his efforts failed. He came back and forth to the kitchen numerous times, just to see if it was time. The clocked seemed to slow down. In his mind, his grandmother delayed more than necessary. The more he concentrated on the cookies, the more he wanted them. It consumed him. When he finally was permitted to get one, it was like a weight had been lifted from his shoulders. The gooey goodness of Grandma's cookies didn't just satisfy his sweet tooth; it warmed his heart because he and Grandma made them together.

- *Question*: What would you identify as the boy's biggest struggle in this scenario?

Scenario Two: Amusement parks weren't his thing; however, he and his wife had promised the children they would take them to one before the summer was over. Today was the day, so they gathered all their daily needs and headed off to what he knew would be a hot and very crowded adventure. The kids were excited, but all he could think about was what he would rather be doing.

When they arrived, the parking lot was so full that they had to park near the back of the lot. His heart sank even further. "If the parking lot is this full, just imagine the number of people inside," he thought, sulking to himself. When they passed through the ticket area, he realized he was right; there were so many people. He was willing to make the best of it for the children's sake, though.

As they rushed to their first ride, the sign above the entrance identified the wait time to be over one hour. His heart sank. "Is this what the rest of the day is going to be like?" With the children and his wife already walking into the line, he followed with a hopeful expectation that the wait time was wrong. He quickly realized the sign didn't lie.

With every small advancement, he grew more and more frustrated. The people behind him were crowding him, the people in front of them wouldn't keep up with the movement of the line, and everyone was being too loud. His children were well behaved, but the energy of the amusement park fueled their level of excitement so much that even they became unusually busy. It was as if his blood was boiling, and his desire to be there grew dimmer with every passing minute.

- *Question*: What is the primary struggle within this man?

If your answer to the first question was that the boy struggled with patience, you are correct. His anticipation for what he knew would be a mouth-wateringly delicious cookie was just about more than he could handle. His grandmother's homemade cookies were the best, and just smelling them baking stretched his patience to its limits.

In the second scenario, you might have said the same thing; however, in the opening sentence, the problem is revealed. He didn't like amusement parks, and the only reason he was there was for the children. The problem was that even doing this for his children was not enough to allow him to enjoy the day. His focus was on everything that was wrong, in his opinion. Ultimately, his focus was on himself and his unhappiness which led him to misery.

As the book of James concludes, we are introduced to the Patient Man in chapter 5. It makes sense why James would wait until the last chapter to introduce this person to us because he serves as the final punctuation to the message. With every command given and every rebuke sternly offered, there is still an underlying truth that Jesus will return and judgment will be rendered. Therefore, James wants these Christians to be patient in their circumstances and with one another as they await.

In James 5:7, we read, "Therefore be patient, brethren, until the coming of the Lord." The word James uses for "patient" is *makrothuméō* and means "to suffer long, be long-suffering, as opposed to hasty anger or punishment."[1] It also carries the idea of enduring and remaining faithful instead of giving up and walking away. It involves exercising understanding and patience towards people. He will command this of the brethren in verses 7 and 8; then in verse 10, he points to the prophets of old as examples to imitate in their suffering and patience. Interestingly, in verse 10, the word "patience" is a noun and carries the meaning of "forbearance, long-suffering, self-restraint before proceeding to action."[2] Avenging oneself is foreign to this concept of patience, even though it might be within one's power to do so; therefore, the admonition to not complain against one another is very fitting.

THE PATIENT MAN...

1) EXPECTS THE LORD'S RETURN

Expectations are motivational—let that soak in just a bit before reading on. An employee who expects a bonus for doing exceptional work on a project might allow that to propel him to put more time into his research, his proposals, and his final presentation. A high school student who knows that getting a high GPA will increase her chances of attaining more significant scholarships in college will allow that expectation to push her through the long nights of studying and the daunting task of writing papers. A wife who has set the expectation before her husband of a romantic evening when he returns home from work will motivate him to make sure he leaves work on time. It's human nature. If we have expectations, and those expectations are positive, they will serve as motivation. In James chapter 5, we see this same concept brought forth when learning from the Patient Man.

In verses 7 and 8, James goes out of his way to emphasize to his readers the impending coming of the Lord. He does so as a source of motivation for the Christians to remain faithful and avoid the pitfalls of quarreling, fighting, conflict, and judgment that are constantly addressed throughout this letter (2:2-4; 4:1-4; 4:11-12). His desire is for them to remain faithful through the trials they face (1:12) and to take ownership of the sin in their lives so they can address it (1:13-16). He wants them to be involved in doing good works as an overflow of their faithfulness (2:14-26) as they grow and live in a manner consistent with heavenly wisdom (3:13-18). All of this occurs in a culture where the rich are oppressing Christians and making life difficult for them. Some of this conflict is seeping into relationships within the Church.

So, what would be the most powerful and motivating message James could relay that would make these Christians choose to continue to remain faithful through suffering? It's got to be bigger than the "reward" of abandoning the faith and giving in to the rich. It's got to be more impressive than the suffering ending or the lust and pleasures being indulged. What could be bigger and more rewarding for these brethren than for the hurt to stop and pleasures to rule? The answer is that Jesus is coming back, and He will make all things right.

This reality regularly rises to the surface throughout the Bible, especially when there is the possibility of Christians losing faith or growing weak in their dedication to the Lord. The day of the Lord is often used to deter negative behavior while at the same time encouraging God-honoring behavior. It's spoken of as being "near" (James 5:8), a term that allows the Christians to know that their rescue is not far off. We see this in James 5:9 when James writes, "Behold, the Judge is standing right at the door." You and I should not understand these descriptions in terms of time. Instead, the message communicated is that the day of the Lord (meaning His return) is an absolute and guaranteed fact. Consider the following passages.

- "I thank my God always concerning you for the grace of God which was given you in Christ Jesus, that in everything you were enriched in Him, in all speech and all knowledge, even as the testimony concerning Christ was confirmed in you, so that you are not lacking in any gift, awaiting eagerly the revelation of our Lord Jesus Christ, who will also confirm you to the end, blameless **in the day of our Lord Jesus Christ**. God is faithful, through whom you were called into fellowship with His Son, Jesus Christ our Lord" (1 Cor. 1:4-9).

- "Now as to the times and the epochs, brethren, you have no need of anything to be written to you. For you yourselves know full well that **the day of the Lord** will come just like a thief in the night. While they are saying, 'Peace and safety!' then destruction will come upon them suddenly like labor pains upon a woman with child, and they will not escape. But you, brethren, are not in darkness, that the day would overtake you like a thief; for you are all sons of light and sons of day. We are not of night nor of darkness; so then let us not sleep as others do, but let us be alert and sober" (1 Thess. 5:1-6).

- "**But the day of the Lord** will come like a thief, in which the heavens will pass away with a roar and the elements will be destroyed with intense heat, and the earth and its works will be burned up. Since all these things are to be destroyed in this way, what sort of people ought you to be in holy conduct and godliness, looking for and hastening the coming of the **day of God**, because of which the heavens will be destroyed by burning, and the elements will melt with intense heat! But according to His promise we are looking for new heavens and a new earth, in which righteousness dwells" (2 Peter 3:10-13).

The Patient Man of James chapter 5 lives with the hopeful expectation that Jesus is coming back. His unwavering belief is that when He does return, there will be vengeance rendered by God on the evil who have oppressed the saints as well as relief given to those who have endured so much for His name (2 Thess. 1:6-8; Rom. 12:19). His belief in the return of Christ is not rooted in negative motives; it's not that he wishes harm on those who do evil. He simply understands what will happen when the Lord returns. The Patient Man is motivated by the day of the Lord much the same way a distance runner is inspired to give a little extra to his pace as he enters the last mile of the race, knowing the finish line is not that far ahead. He can push through the pain and exhaustion. Likewise, the Christian who is patient decides he can be more long-suffering and less reactive to frustrations or oppression from others. The Patient Man serves as a wonderful example of what it means to "hasten the day of the Lord" (2 Peter 3:12).

The Patient Man of James chapter 5 lives with the hopeful expectation that Jesus is coming back.

2) STRENGTHENS HIS HEART

To be honest, this aspect of the Patient Man of James chapter 5 appeals to me. The main reason is that I understand the concept of physically strengthening oneself very well. A regular routine of lifting weights increases strength as the muscle fibers are broken down and rebuilt repeatedly. Most of us understand this because we live and exist in the flesh. We've been taught through school and society the importance of health and wellness, so maybe we take for granted that if strengthening occurs, then energy must be exerted. Sitting around and being lazy doesn't get it done, so if we are going to become stronger, it's up to us.

What about strengthening the heart, as referred to in James 5:8? How does that happen? While we use this phrase or idea in our culture, I'm curious how many truly know what it means, much less how to go about achieving it.

In the Bible, the heart is often used to refer to the inner person. This is where thoughts occur, decisions are made, and actions are born. This is the aspect of mankind that the Pharisees seemed to overlook for the sake of outward actions. Jesus, however, taught that the heart was extremely important to God (Matt. 5:5-7). When we read these and other passages of Scripture, we can clearly see the vital importance of the heart as defined and used in the Bible.

- "These words, which I am commanding you today, shall be on your heart (Deut. 6:6).
- "Let the words of my mouth and the meditation of my heart Be acceptable in Your sight, O Lord, my rock and my Redeemer" (Psalm 19:14).
- "Wait for the Lord; Be strong and let your heart take courage; Yes, wait for the Lord" (Psalm 27:14).
- "Make your ear attentive to wisdom, incline your heart to understanding" (Prov. 2:2).
- "Watch over your heart with all diligence, For from it flow the springs of life" (Prov. 4:23).
- "For out of the heart come evil thoughts, murders, adulteries, fornications, thefts, false witness, slanders" (Matt. 15:19).
- "But thanks be to God that though you were slaves of sin, you became obedient from the heart to that form of teaching to which you were committed" (Rom. 6:17).
- "So, as those who have been chosen of God, holy and beloved, put on a heart of compassion, kindness, humility, gentleness and patience" (Col. 3:12).

Therefore, when James writes that the Christians are to strengthen their hearts in James 5:8, he is not talking about their physical, beating hearts. He is talking about this inner man. He's commanding them to strengthen themselves internally with a mental fortitude and direction that cannot be swayed to unfaithfulness.

Unlike lifting weights, where the individual works to strengthen himself, the Bible teaches that one must not trust in himself to grow stronger. The writer of Proverbs said as much when he wrote, "Trust in the Lord with all your heart and do not lean on your own understanding. In all your ways acknowledge Him, and He will make your paths straight" (Prov. 3:5-6). The strength we gain as followers of Jesus Christ is not based upon our strength. The minute we begin boasting in our heritage, accomplishments, and actions, we have lost the most important anchor in our lives, knowing Christ (Phil. 3:1-11). Since we are to rely entirely on Jesus as the single source of strength, how can we strengthen ourselves?

> *The strength we gain as followers of Jesus Christ is not based upon our strength.*

To understand this, we must define what is meant by "strengthen." The word used by inspiration of the Holy Spirit in James 5:8 is the word *stērízō* and means "to set fast, to fix firmly."[3] When referring to people, it means to be steadfast in mind or unwavering in mind. This understanding draws us back to what James said in 1:7-8 when he wrote, "For that man ought not to expect that he will receive anything from the Lord, being a double-minded man, unstable in all his ways." God expects His children to anchor the inner man, his mind and beliefs; this is the strengthening of the heart. It doesn't mean that you are the source of your own strength. Rather, you are to set your heart, your inner being, on God in such a fixated manner that you will be able to endure whatever trials (1:2) you encounter.

This doesn't happen by accident but is intentional. The Patient Man of James chapter 5 teaches us this can only occur when staying focused on Christ. The truth is, where you look is where you'll go, and if you focus on the difficulties, your mind will always dwell there. That's why the writer of Hebrews encouraged single-minded focus on Jesus when writing,

> *Therefore, since we have so great a cloud of witnesses surrounding us, let us also lay aside every encumbrance and the sin which so easily entangles us, and let us run with endurance the race that is set before us, fixing our eyes on Jesus, the author and perfecter of faith, who for the joy set before*

Him endured the cross, despising the shame, and has sat down at the right hand of the throne of God. For consider Him who has endured such hostility by sinners against Himself, so that you will not grow weary and lose heart. (Heb. 12:1-3)

The Patient Man also teaches us that strengthening one's heart can only occur when the Christian leans on God through an active and faithful prayer life. The word "pray" or "prayer" occurs seven times from verses 13-20. The significance of this frequency after James commanded patience cannot be overemphasized. As a matter of fact, the tremendous stress placed on prayer only solidifies the fact that if Christians are going to be patient and strengthen their hearts, they have to lean on and trust in God and His will. He took care of the prophets (5:10) and Job (5:11), so the Patient Man trusts that God will take care of him as well.

3) DOES NOT COMPLAIN

When one is placed in the arena of discomfort or the pressure cooker of trials, grumbling and complaining seem to be the natural reaction. When the children of Israel were rescued from Egyptian bondage and had to journey through the wilderness, the Bible says they grumbled about everything from food to water to the amount of time Moses spent on Mt. Sinai. They even wished they had been left in Egypt to die (Exod. 15:24; 16:2-3). When the twelves spies returned to Moses, they reported that the people in the land were strong, the cities were fortified and very large, and there were a significant number of tribes living in the land who would put up a fight. What was the result of this negative report? The people of Israel again grumbled and complained (Num. 13:25-33). Even in the New Testament, we see this same reaction when Jesus went to eat at the house of Zacchaeus. The Pharisees observed this and the Bible informs us they began to grumble saying, "He has gone to be the guest of a man who is a sinner" (Luke 19:7). This is the same reaction the Pharisees displayed in Luke 15:2 as Jesus welcomed tax collectors and sinners and ate with them.

Perhaps the best passage in the New Testament that speaks to the issue of grumbling, and reveals the sources of it, is the parable of the laborers in the vineyard from Matthew chapter 20. As Jesus teaches what the kingdom of heaven will be like, He describes those hired to work at various hours throughout the day. All were paid the same amount; it's what they all agreed to when they were hired. When those who had been working all day saw what those who had only worked an hour were getting, they thought they would be paid more when the landowner got around to paying them (20:10). However, they all received exactly what they had agreed to at the beginning of the day. At this point, Jesus says, "When they received it, they grumbled at the landowner, saying, 'These last men have worked only one hour, and you have made them equal to us who have borne the burden and the scorching heat of the day'" (Matt. 20:11-12). Jesus' ultimate lesson from this parable is seen in verse 16 regarding the first being last and the last being first. However, for our purpose in this chapter, I want us to consider why these workers grumbled.

Initially, these workers were pleased with going to work for a denarius. This was the going rate for a day's work. There was nothing more they should have expected; after all, when they agreed, there was no greater obligation on the landowner's part. It wasn't until they saw the wages of those who had not worked as long and hard as they did that they had a problem. They thought things would be different. They thought that surely the landowner was going to increase their wages. When that didn't happen, they felt an injustice had been done, and they spoke up to try to make it right. There was no injustice, though. What they had once been happy being paid was no longer good enough. Because they compared what they received to what the latecomers received, they became disgruntled and grumbled.

In chapter 5, verse 9, James instructed the Christians, "Do not complain, brethren, against one another, so that you yourselves may not be judged; behold, the Judge is standing right at the door." Emphasis on the relationships between Christians has been apparent throughout this entire letter. The oppression that existed from the rich in chapter 2 and the insults that were hurled by the uncontrolled tongues of the teachers in chapter 3 no doubt presented an abundance of opportunities for disdain, discomfort, and complaint. Perhaps many of those who felt the pressure, pain, stress, or anger these opportunities created often sought some sort of a release, like letting off steam. Maybe those on the receiving end of the steam were family and friends, brothers and sisters in Christ. That's why James warns the Christians not to complain against one another. He reminds them that they are not the judge of one another, as that task belongs to the Judge who is standing at the door.

The Patient Man of chapter 5 teaches us that being patient also means doing so without lashing out in anger or grumbling because of suffering. To be patient means to be focused on Christ and not oneself. A self-focused outlook on life stands opposed to a Christ-centered focus. When we focus on our discomforts, we, like the children of Israel, often fall into complaining and grumbling. God demands different; we need to be different.

> *A self-focused outlook on life stands opposed to a Christ-centered focus.*

CONCLUSION

The farmer is unquestionably one of the best illustrations of patience. His entire lifestyle is centered around doing daily work that has no immediate return. The soil is prepared, the seed is sown, and the crop finally comes in during harvest time. Think about the cattle farmer. He feeds his animals every day and ensures that they have the proper medicines to prevent worms or diseases. It takes a long time to get a cow up to weight before he can sell it at the auction for the highest offer. The common theme seen in farming is doing a lot of work with no pay in order to get paid when the harvest comes. If a farmer doesn't do the work without receiving immediate payment, he will never receive compensation during harvest.

In James 5:7, we see that the farmer illustrates the ideal way to have a mental image of what patience looks like. There are many things the farmer can control; however, even in his preparation, he can't control the weather. He can no more control the sunshine or the rain than he can control when Jesus is going to come again. All he can do is wait and remain steadfast in doing the work he can control. In the same way, the Patient Man of James 5 teaches us to be long-suffering as we work in this life to bring glory to God. There were opportunities for the Christians who received this letter from James to give up and give in, surrendering to the difficulties in life. We, too, regularly face the same decision. What we learn from the Patient Man is that by keeping our focus on Christ and His return, strengthening our hearts, and encouraging our brothers and sisters in Christ, we can do more than simply hold on. We can actually have abundant joy through this life, regardless of the trials we encounter (James 1:2).

REFLECTION QUESTIONS

1. Why is patience such a big struggle for some? In what ways does struggling with patience cause problems in marriages, between parents/children, brothers and sisters in Christ, and possibly in your work?

2. How does living with the expectation of Jesus return help motivate you? Specifically, what difference has been made in your life because you are living with the expectation of Jesus' returning?

3. Since you are to rely entirely on Jesus as the single source of strength, how can you strengthen yourself? What are some practical ways you can begin to do this today?

4. Why do people complain? What do they hope to gain from doing so?

5. Instead of complaining about the difficulties of following Christ, how can you use the trials you encounter to draw you closer to Christ and lead others to the Lord?

ENDNOTES

CHAPTER 1
1. *The Complete Word Study Dictionary: New Testament*, 2000, s.v. "hupomenei."
2. *The Complete Word Study Dictionary: New Testament*, 2000, s.v. "peirasmós."

CHAPTER 2
1. https://www.merriam-webster.com/dictionary/science
2. https://www.merriam-webster.com/dictionary/physics
3. https://byjus.com/physics/law-of-inertia
4. *Greek-English Lexicon of the New Testament*, 2nd ed., s.v. "personal favoritism."
5. *The Complete Word Study Dictionary: New Testament*, 2000, s.v. "agapáō."
6. *The Complete Word Study Dictionary: New Testament*, 2000, s.v. "mercy."
7. *Baker Encyclopedia of the Bible*, s.v. "disciple."

CHAPTER 3
1. *The Complete Word Study Dictionary: New Testament*, 2000, s.v. "be diligent."
2. https://www.merriam-webster.com/dictionary/eager
3. *The Complete Word Study Dictionary: New Testament*, 2000, s.v. "hypocrisy."
4. Mariam Arain, et al, "Maturation of the Adolescent Brain," *Neuropsychiatric Disease and Treatment* (Dove Medical Press, 2013), https://www.ncbi.nlm.nih.gov/pmc/articles/PMC3621648/
5. *The Complete Word Study Dictionary: New Testament*, 2000, s.v. "righteousness."

CHAPTER 4
1. *The Complete Word Study Dictionary: New Testament*, 2000, s.v. "pleasures."
2. *The Complete Word Study Dictionary: New Testament*, 2000, s.v. "lust."
3. *The Complete Word Study Dictionary: New Testament*, 2000, s.v. "envious."
4. *The Complete Word Study Dictionary: New Testament*, 2000, s.v. "submission."
5. http://www.sermonillustrations.com/a-z/h/humility.htm

CHAPTER 5
1. *The Complete Word Study Dictionary: New Testament*, 2000, s.v. "patient."
2. *The Complete Word Study Dictionary: New Testament*, 2000, s.v. "patience."
3. *The Complete Word Study Dictionary: New Testament*, 2000, s.v. "strengthen."

www.ingramcontent.com/pod-product-compliance
Lightning Source LLC
Chambersburg PA
CBHW041132110526
44592CB00020B/2775